Is The Bib .

The Book of Ruth and Biblical Narrative

Richard Bauckham

Professor of New Testament Studies, St Mary's College,
University of St Andrews

GROVE BOOKS LIMITED
RIDLEY HALL RD CAMBRIDGE CB3 9HU

Contents

The Cover Illustration is by Peter Ashton

First Impression December 1996
ISSN 1365-490X
ISBN 1 85174 331 6

1

Introduction

Feminist biblical criticism is an important current in contemporary study of the Bible. Undeniably it has raised our consciousness about a series of questions which professional interpretation of the Bible (whether in the pulpit or in academic scholarship) has commonly ignored, mainly, as we can now see, because it was almost entirely done by male interpreters who unthinkingly read the texts within a masculine horizon of interests. Women who now come to the texts with questions raised by the feminist movement are not only asking new questions but also thereby enabling us to see whole new dimensions of the meaning of the texts. However controversial some of the results may be, male and female readers of Scripture alike have much to gain from escaping the dominance of masculine concerns in the interpretation of Scripture.

Feminist Criticism

There is a wide range of broadly feminist approaches to the interpretation of the Bible, some much more akin to traditional interpretative approaches, some reflecting the most radical forms of feminist theory. But all truly feminist approaches are inescapably *critical*—that is, they are critical of the structures and ideologies of male dominance. Applied to the Bible, they cannot but raise for us the question: Is not the Bible a male book? Is not the Bible, like most of the literature produced by the patriarchal societies of the past, a book written by men, reflecting male experience, adopting a male perspective, supporting, implicitly and explicitly, the male-dominated social structures by which men oppress women? Is it not one of the most dangerous of male books, since it has been accorded such authority and allowed such influence over the thinking and the lives of both men and women? This question is naturally disturbing to those who are accustomed to seek in the Bible, not a male perspective, but God's perspective on human life. The Bible has been called 'the Word of God in the words of men'—where 'men' is intended in the (now old-fashioned) generic sense of 'human beings.' But if these words of 'men' are in fact the words of male human beings, written from a male perspective, advocating male interests against the interests of women, we may rightly wonder how far they can embody the Word of God. The feminist critique of the Bible as a male book raises disturbing questions which need to be squarely faced. Facing them may lead us behind the tradition of dominantly male interpretation of the Bible to rediscover some respects in which the Bible is not so exclusively male after all.

The criticism of the Bible as male is not as simple as it may first appear. It can be divided into two main charges: *patriarchalism* and *androcentrism*.

Patriarchalism

Most discussion of feminist issues in interpretation of the Bible has focused on the charge that the Bible is patriarchal—that is, the Bible is said to *reflect the structures of male authority* in the societies in which it originated. More importantly, it is said to *endorse and to promote these oppressive structures by which men dominate and exploit women.* The debatable questions here concern the extent to which the Bible does support such structures and the extent to which key elements in the biblical literature in fact resist or oppose such structures. There are passages which affirm the fundamental equality of women and men in creation (Gen 1.27) and redemption (Gal 3.28), and those which show women exercising leadership roles in the earliest churches alongside men (eg Rom 16.7). These can be the keys to a feminist hermeneutic (method of reading and interpreting) which perceives and follows a biblical direction towards the liberation of women from male domination and the affirmation of women's full equality with men in every sphere of society. However, our present concern is not primarily with patriarchal structures. Extremely important though this question is, our present concern is different. It is with the *androcentrism* of Scripture, an element in the feminist critique of Scripture which is rather less often discussed but fully deserving of attention in its own right.

Androcentrism

The claim that the biblical literature is androcentric (a term which means 'centred on men'; the corresponding term meaning 'centred on women' is 'gynocentric') suggests that this literature not only reflects the patriarchal structures of the societies in which it was written, but is also written from the perspective of men in those societies. In reading the texts we see their world from a male perspective, focusing on male interests, oblivious to the concerns of women in those societies. If we do not notice this male perspective, it is because we have been seduced into treating it as a universal perspective, as men themselves frequently do. Once alerted to issues of gender and to the differences of roles and interests which women and men have in patriarchal societies, we begin to recognize the extent to which the perspective of the texts is male-dominated. If we think, for example, of the narrative literature of the Old Testament, it is obvious that the majority of the characters are male, that activities such as war and politics (which were almost exclusively male activities in ancient Israel) take up much space, and that even when women appear in the narratives they are often viewed from the perspective of the male characters. Moreover, the more we are inclined to see the patriarchal societies from which the literature comes as oppressive to women, the more disturbing will be the claim that the literature provides us with the perspective of the oppressors, and not that of the oppressed. Androcentrism is clearly more problematic in a patriarchal society than it would be in an egalitarian society which did not privilege the interests of men over those of women.

The Place of Women-Centred Narratives

The issues of patriarchy and androcentrism are thus connected, but in principle distinguishable. By focusing in this booklet on the problem of androcentrism we shall find ourselves also dealing with the problem of patriarchy to an extent, but only to a limited extent. Any idea that the argument presented here meets the feminist charge that the Bible supports patriarchy would be quite mistaken. That is not our aim here. But feminist challenges to traditional exegetical assumptions are too wide-ranging to be met by some quick and easy response. Different issues need adequate attention in their own right. Our present concern is with androcentrism, and more specifically with androcentrism in biblical *narratives*. The issue of androcentrism in other kinds of biblical literature—for example, prophetic literature or wisdom literature—takes rather different forms and cannot be pursued here. Narrative literature offers the most promising scope for an initial exploration of the issue. This is because, as we shall argue, it is possible to identify clearly gynocentric narratives within the biblical literature. Though biblical narratives are predominantly androcentric, there are significant gynocentric interruptions of the dominant male perspective. Sometimes the texts permit us to see the biblical world from the perspective of biblical women. When we recognize this difference between androcentric and gynocentric narratives, then we can ask how the gynocentric exceptions can function, for readers of Scripture, in relation to the androcentric perspective of the majority of biblical narratives. Are they merely occasional exceptions which leave the dominant androcentrism undisturbed, or do they in fact challenge and relativize the dominant androcentrism? Appreciation of the women's perspective of some biblical narratives may affect the way one reads the androcentric narratives.

The Book of Ruth

Among the Old Testament narratives, the book of Ruth provides the clearest and most interesting example of a deliberate and sustained adoption of a gynocentric perspective on ancient Israelite life. This biblical book arguably has, as part of its purpose, precisely the balancing and correcting of the male perspective of most Old Testament narrative by means of a female perspective. Admittedly, until recently, almost all professional interpretation of the book of Ruth has been interested in anything and everything about this text *apart from* its obvious gynocentrism, though one suspects that the latter has not been lost on ordinary Jewish and Christian women who have read the text. Moreover, we cannot simply take it for granted that a text whose two main characters are women is genuinely gynocentric. Such a text could project a male view of women, not truly reflective of women's real experience and concerns. But recent study, adopting feminist approaches, has tended to the view that the book shows good evidence of genuinely reflecting the experience of women in ancient Israelite and convincingly adopting an Israelite women's perspective on ancient Israelite society. (Of course, it is essential not to reify 'women's experience' and 'women's perspective,' as though these were the same in all cultural contexts. They relate to specific cultures, in which, among other things, the roles and relations of men and women vary. In this case, it is the experience and perspective of women in ancient Israel that are at issue.) Recent writers have therefore identified Ruth as 'a female text'[1] or 'a collective creation of women's culture'[2] or 'an expression of women's culture and women's concerns.'[3]

Gender and Authorship

Calling Ruth 'a female text' or 'women's literature' does not necessarily imply that it was written by a woman, though this is a possibility that certainly cannot be ruled out. A word about female authorship in Scripture is appropriate at this point, since one element in the claim that the Bible is a male book is sometimes the assumption that it was written entirely by men. This assumption, which traditional, male-dominated biblical interpretation has usually made in the past, should not go unchallenged. We know that ancient Israelite women composed songs, that there were women prophets in Israel and the early church, that women in ancient Israel sometimes gave wisdom instruction, and that there were women apostles and teachers in the earliest Christian churches. There is no reason at all why such women should not have contributed significantly to the formation of the biblical literature. Only a few passages of Scripture actually claim female authorship (for example, 1 Sam 2.1-10 and Prov 31), but much of Scripture (including Ruth) is anonymous. And since much of the biblical literature incorporates traditions which had a long history prior to their incorporation in the books we have, women may have played important roles in the oral origins and transmission of the contents of the Bible even if they had little part in compiling and composing the texts in their final form. If authorship of Scripture is understood in a broad sense—the people who contributed significantly to the making of these books—then it must be virtually certain that women played a part, though we cannot really estimate its extent.

On the other hand, it is also important to insist that literature written by men can genuinely reflect women's experience, just as literature written by women can genuinely reflect men's experience. Modern novels are probably the best examples of this. Some (not all) creative writers of imaginative literature are capable of profoundly entering the experience of people of the opposite sex, just as they can enter the experience of people in very different cultural and life situations from their own, and can portray characters of the opposite sex in such

---

1   A Brenner, 'Introduction,' in A Brenner (ed), *A Feminist Companion to Ruth* (Sheffield: Sheffield Academic Press, 1993) p 14; C Meyers, 'Returning Home: Ruth 1.8 and the Gendering of the Book of Ruth,' in Brenner, *Ruth*, p 114.
2   F van Dijk-Hemmes, 'Ruth: A Product of Women's Culture?' in Brenner, *Ruth*, p 139.
3   A Brenner, 'Naomi and Ruth: Further Reflections' in Brenner, *Ruth*, p 143.

a way that readers of that sex can authentically identify with such characters. Most would agree that some of the ancient Greek dramatists, who were all male, successfully portray women's experience and a women's perspective on society. We need not deny to male biblical authors a similar imaginative capacity. One factor which facilitated this in the ancient world was oral storytelling, which often takes place in a context in which audiences react and participate. A skilled storyteller relating to audiences composed of both women and men learns to depict characters of both sexes whom members of the audience recognize as true to their own experience. Thus, even if a biblical narrative such as Ruth is a product of storytelling by men, the women characters will have been, as it were, tested on audiences including women and even formed partly through the participation of women in the audiences. The authenticity of women's experience and perspective in a narrative need not imply a female author.

There is no way of knowing whether the author of Ruth was male or female, and the issue is not in itself important. What we can say is that the *voice* with which this text speaks to its readers is female. Readers are offered and drawn into an ancient Israelite women's perspective on ancient Israelite society. It is with the aim of appreciating this perspective that we now turn to the story the book tells.

2
What is the Story of Ruth About?

In order to appreciate the way in which the book of Ruth provides an Israelite women's perspective on ancient Israelite society, we need first to understand the major themes and concerns of the story it tells.

Theme 1: Naomi's Economic Security

Like many good stories, the plot of the book poses a problem at the beginning and resolves the problem at the end. The problem is Naomi's need for economic security. *The story is about how Naomi acquires economic security.* Primarily it is *Naomi's* need that is the theme, since, despite its title, the book is in fact more Naomi's story than it is Ruth's. The story begins and ends with Naomi. The summary of her life thus far in the first five verses of the book sets up a situation in which Naomi is left without husband or sons. In such a society this means that she is without any secure form of economic support. In the simple agrarian society of early Israel, each family makes a basic living from its own plot of land. Naomi in fact owns land in Bethlehem, which she has inherited from her dead husband Elimelech, since he has no male heirs. She can own it until there is a male heir. But the story takes for granted that Naomi is unable to farm her land and make a living from it herself, even with Ruth's help. This may be simply because women in ancient Israel, though they shared in some agricultural work, never did the principal tasks involved in growing crops. In any case, Naomi, although she owns land, is in the situation common to women who had no male relative to provide for them. She is one of 'the poor' who have no economic security but survive from hand to mouth. So chapter 1 stresses the *bitterness* of Naomi's desperate situation, which she blames on God (1.13, 20-21). This is the problem the plot contrives to solve. By the end of the story Ruth has achieved for Naomi the economic security she needs. Ruth bears a son, whom the women of Bethlehem describe as Naomi's son (4.17). The sense in which Obed is Naomi's son is that of providing for her economic security (4.15: 'a restorer of life and a nourisher of your old age'). The story which begins with Naomi's economic plight ends with the achievement of her economic security.

Ruth, of course, plays a key role in this. She gives up the chance of economic security (cf 1.9) which she could have by staying in Moab and marrying again, and opts instead to accompany Naomi to Bethlehem, where she has not much chance of marrying again. She sacrifices her own chance of security for Naomi's sake. But in Bethlehem Ruth's own efforts to support Naomi and herself by gleaning at harvest-time combine with Naomi's concern to secure Ruth's future (3.1) to produce, in the event, a secure future for them both, when Ruth marries Boaz and bears a son. The two women, by their mutual concern and support, succeed in achieving economic security for them both.

Modern western readers do not always notice the story's emphasis on economic security, preferring to focus on less material elements in the relationships of the characters. But Ruth is a story close to the realities of life in a peasant society with a subsistence economy. In a society in which every family household owned and farmed its own land, most people had a very basic but dependable livelihood. Unless there were serious famine (like that to which Ruth 1.1 refers) or some other disaster, most people had economic security at a basic level. But inevitably there were those who fell outside this system. Those who could not farm their own land, who therefore had no security, who lived from hand to mouth, not knowing where the next day's meal was coming from, were the poor. Economic security, at however basic a level of subsistence, was what distinguished most people from the poor, who had no such security. So the typical categories of the poor, who frequently appear in the biblical literature, are widows, orphans and sojourners (resident aliens). Resident aliens could not own land, widows and orphans could not farm it themselves, even if they owned some. Naomi and Ruth are both widows, while Ruth is also a resident alien. They belong to the classic categories of people who are needy because they lack economic security. The story tells how they acquire it.

Theme 2: Women's Solidarity and Resourcefulness

Ruth is *a story about women's solidarity and resourcefulness in securing their future against the odds.* They succeed because they are committed and devoted to each other, concerned for each other's interests. This commitment is memorably expressed in Ruth's famous words, vowing her loyalty to Naomi in whatever circumstances, near the beginning of the story (1.16-17), and also in the words of the women of Bethlehem, at the end of the story, calling Ruth Naomi's 'daughter-in-law who loves you, who is more to you than seven sons' (4.15). The two women succeed through their loyal cooperation with each other. They also succeed because they act with independence and initiative, within the very restricted options their society gives them. Notably, Ruth in effect proposes marriage to Boaz (3.6-9), following Naomi's suggestion that she do so (3.1-4). The decisive action in the plot, Boaz's marrying Ruth, derives from an initiative which is in the first place Naomi's and then Ruth's, and to which Boaz responds. Of course, Boaz's willingness to marry Ruth is also essential to the plot. He is not tricked or induced into the marriage, but is genuinely delighted that Ruth wishes to marry him (3.10). But the initiative comes from the women, not from him.

Theme 3: The Covenant Society

While Ruth is very much a story about women's solidarity and resourcefulness in securing their future against the odds, it is not, as some feminist interpreters would wish, a story of women resisting a patriarchal society and succeeding in spite of it. This is not how the book presents the matter. Rather, in the context of the laws and ideals of ancient Israel, Ruth is *a story about how the covenant society ought to operate for the benefit of those most in need.*

There are two aspects to this. The first is that the society has certain legal provisions designed to support those who fall outside the regular means of economic subsistence, in other words those who do not own land or cannot work the land, typically the widows, the orphans and the resident aliens. There is, for example, the law of gleaning, which is not a form of voluntary charity on the part of farmers, but a legal requirement that some of the harvest be left for the poor to gather (Lev 19.9; 23.22; Deut 24.19). When Ruth gleans in Boaz's field, she exercises her legal right as a resident alien. The laws of redemption and levirate marriage (cf Lev 25.23-31; Deut 25.5-10) enabled a widow who had no son to secure her future by marrying and bearing a son who could then inherit her first husband's property. Though the precise legal arrangements which in the story enable Ruth's marriage to Boaz and the inheritance of Elimelech's land by her son (4.1-10) are obscure, they certainly constitute a case of such laws operating to the benefit of a widow in Ruth's position (and, in this case, also a widow in Naomi's position). Finally, the law required that the resident alien be treated equally with the native Israelite (Lev 19.33-34).

Loving Faithfulness

The second aspect is that, although these provisions exist in the legal framework that governs the life of God's covenant people, they only operate for the benefit of Naomi and Ruth because Naomi, Ruth and Boaz actually make them so operate. What makes the legal provisions operate for the benefit of those intended to benefit from them is people's *hesed*, a word which is usually, in Ruth, translated 'kindness' or 'loyalty.' It refers to the caring responsibility which people show for each other. Ruth acts with *hesed* towards Naomi (cf 2.11), Naomi acts with *hesed* towards Ruth, Ruth acts with *hesed* towards Boaz (3.10), and Boaz responds with *hesed*.

Thus the two women act with initiative and self-determination and secure their own future, but they do not do so against the grain of the structures of the covenant society. It is rather that, by acting with *hesed* and when Boaz responds with *hesed*, they make those structures designed for their advantage actually work for their advantage.

Theme 4: God's Covenant Loyalty

Finally, Ruth is *a story of God's hesed or covenant loyalty to his people.* God is quite frequently mentioned as the source of the good that comes to Ruth and Naomi. But God does not intervene in any way other than acting, implicitly, through the human characters. God's *hesed* (2.20) takes effect through being reflected in the human *hesed* of Ruth, Naomi and Boaz. So the story tells how the provisions God has made for his people in his law prove a blessing when his people act with *hesed* that reflects his own *hesed*. The 'idyllic' quality which has often been noticed in the book of Ruth can be exaggerated, since the story begins with famine, exile, death, destitution and Naomi's bitter complaints that the Lord has turned against her and dealt harshly with her. The idyllic quality only gradually colours the narrative as it proceeds, and as God is found to be after all gracious and kind (2.12, 20; 4.14). It corresponds to the way the provisions God has made for his covenant people take effect in the kindness and caring responsibility of people. The setting of the story 'in the days when the judges ruled' (1.1) makes it, as it were, a contrast and counter-example to the closing chapters of the book of Judges (19-21). There, outrageous acts of violation of covenant responsibilities, in events as local and particular as those in Ruth, lead to genocidal civil war and the near-extinction of a whole tribe in Israel. Against the horrors of the last chapters of Judges the book of Ruth sets an attractive picture of community life in Israel as it could be when God's provisions and intentions for his people are implemented and reflected in human *hesed*.

3
The Women's Perspective in Ruth

We are now in position to appreciate the way the book of Ruth not only tells the story of two women, Naomi and Ruth, but also does this in such a way as to open up for its readers a distinctively and authentically women's perspective on ancient Israelite society. Paradoxically, readers become most consciously aware of this when the women's perspective is briefly superseded by a male perspective on the same events. Deliberately putting the two perspectives side by side makes it unequivocally clear that there are two *different* perspectives, and that it is the women's perspective which predominates.

From the death of Elimelech (1.3) onwards, the story adopts the perspective of Naomi and subsequently also of Ruth. But there is one major interruption of this women's perspective. Necessarily, in this society, the legal transaction—involving both the redemption of Naomi's land and the related obligation to marry Ruth—takes place among the men of Bethlehem (4.1-12). The scene is set in the city gate, where Boaz sits with the elders—all male, of course—who constitute the city's legal authority. There Boaz exercises his legal right, once it has been ceded him by the nearer kinsman who has first claim, to redeem the land and to marry the widow whose son will thus be able to inherit it. Thereby Elimelech's land is kept in the kinship group. So in Boaz's legal declaration (4.9-10) and in the people's congratulation of him (4.11-12) we are given the male perspective on his marriage to Ruth. It concerns the provision of a male heir for Elimelech and Mahlon (4.9-10)—'to maintain the dead man's name on his inheritance, in order that the name of the dead may not be cut off from his kindred and from the gate of his native place' (4.10)—and also the provision of children for Boaz himself (4.11-12): 'May you produce children in Ephrathah and bestow a name in Bethlehem' (4.11).

The hopes expressed in this male scene at the city gate are fulfilled in the birth of a son to Ruth and Boaz. But this event is the occasion for the women of Bethlehem to express, in their congratulation of Naomi and at their naming of Obed (4.14-15, 17), the corresponding and very different female perspective. The same events which readers have just viewed from the male perspective, voiced by Boaz and the people at the gate, are now presented from the female perspective. For the women the child is Naomi's son (4.17). This is not because he is her son or even grandson in a biological sense, but because he will be the security for her old age that she thought she had lost when her own sons died. And she owes him to her 'daughter-in-law who loves you, who is more to you than seven sons' (4.15). From the women's perspective what has happened is not that Boaz has acquired an heir for Elimelech, but that Ruth's devotion to Naomi has secured a son to be Naomi's support in her old age. From both perspectives the continuity of life into a third generation is secured and from both perspectives the biological links also serve non-biological connections, but the concern for patrilineal descent, biological or legal, which dominates one perspective is wholly absent from the other.

We should also note that the change of perspective accompanies a change of scene, from the city gate where the men transact legal affairs and seem to themselves to play the dominant role in society, securing the continuity of the male line across the generations, to the household, where the women manage the continuity of the generations, not in legal but in practical and affective terms, and seem to themselves to be the real actors in events of significance.

How the Perspectives Relate

The women's perspective in 4.14-17 clearly completes the overall perspective of the narrative of the book. It carries through the concerns of the first three chapters, whereas concern for the continuance of Elimelech's line has no place at all in the book until Boaz sits with the elders in the gate. The men's concerns expressed in the scene at the gate interrupt the women's concerns which have dominated the first three chapters and which are resumed in the scene following the birth of Obed. The men's perspective corresponds to the form of the legal process, which is essential to the narrative, but the female perspective is no less true to the substance of what actually happens. The narrative gives the men's perspective voice in order to replace it by the women's perspective.

This does not mean that it invalidates the men's perspective as such. What Boaz says the legal transaction does for the relation of property to family structures it really does, and what the people wish for Boaz he really gains. The men's perspective is not illusory in what it claims, merely one-sided in what it leaves out. It does not touch the significance of the events for the women. Taken by itself, as though it were a universal perspective, it gives a misleading impression of the dominance of masculine concerns, which the mere juxtaposition of the women's perspective is sufficient to dispel.

Thus the book of Ruth is not polemical or adversarial towards men. The only male character portrayed in detail, Boaz, is portrayed entirely positively. But the book does protest, as it were, against any assumption that the men's perspective on the world of ancient Israel is sufficient or universal or the same as the women's. It shows up the limited character of the male perspective that more usually dominates the narratives of the Hebrew scriptures. By juxtaposing it with a (for once) more dominant female perspective, it shows the latter to be different and at least equally valid. It allows readers of the Old Testament narratives to enter and to appreciate the perspective of their female characters.

Among other things the contrast of perspectives says that the legal conventions of patrilineal descent and inheritance, despite their patriarchal form, can operate in practice as structures for women just as much as for men. Seen only from the men's perspective they seem more patriarchal than they are.

Internal Dynamics

An incidental but interesting indication of the women's perspective on the structures of Israelite society which the book of Ruth adopts is the phrase 'mother's house' in 1.8. The phrase occurs in only three other verses of the Hebrew Bible (Gen 24.28; Cant 3.4; 8.2), but the same social reality it describes appears frequently in the Hebrew Bible as the 'father's house.' It is the basic social and economic unit of ancient Israelite society: the family household. The phrase 'mother's house' describes from the female perspective the social institution which is usually viewed from the male perspective as the 'father's house.' The latter description might lead us to suppose that the ancient Israelite household was a thoroughly patriarchal institution, dominated by the male head of the household. In fact, Carol Meyers' important work[4] on early Israelite society, drawing on archeological and anthropological as well as biblical evidence, shows that this was not the case. The ancient Israelite household, she argues, was 'characterized by internal gender balance rather than gender hierarchy:'

'The word "internal" is critical here. Whereas outward forms of status and recognition may indicate male privilege, the dynamics within domestic units may be quite different, with women even dominating the multifarious facets of economic life, and also the social and parenting activities, that take place within the family household. Because the public record of ancient Israel, like that of most traditional societies, is so androcentric, aspects of female power within the Israelite household can rarely be seen. Yet the relative invisibility of female power does not mean it did not exist; and occasionally it can be glimpsed even in the male-oriented canon.'[5]

Meyers' study of the texts (including Ruth) which use the term 'mother's house' affords one glimpse of the internal world of the household from the women's perspective, revealing that 'within that setting, women's voices were heard, their presence was valuable and valued, and their deeds had a profound influence on others.'[6] She is also careful to insist that one should not interpret this female power within the household in terms of a modern distinction between private and public, which is not appropriate to ancient societies in which the household and the workplace were virtually identical. Family life was not 'distinct from the general social relations involved in economic, political and religious life.'[7] So the fact that women's roles were largely internal to the household does not mean that the power and influence of women was confined to a private sphere of society contrasted, in modern terms, with the public world. The ancient Isra-

4   See C Meyers, *Discovering Eve: Ancient Israelite Women in Context* (New York/Oxford: Oxford University Press, 1988).
5   C Meyers, 'Returning Home,' p 99.
6   Ibid p 111.
7   Ibid pp 111-112.

elite household was much the most important social and economic structure in ancient Israelite society.

The model drawn from anthropological study which Meyers uses to illuminate the world of ancient Israel is that of a peasant society which is patriarchal in its formal structures of authority, but much less male-dominated in day-to-day reality. In such a society the idea of male dominance is embodied in public displays of male authority. But social reality at the all-important level of the household is characterized by an absence of hierarchical gender relationships and a balance of male and female power. 'Male authority [is] offset by female power.'[8] A critical distinction between authority and power is at stake here. Authority is 'the culturally legitimated right to make decisions and command obedience,' whereas power is 'the ability to effect control despite or independent of official authority... Authority is basically a hierarchical arrangement that may be expressed in formal legal or juridical traditions. Power has no such cultural sanctions but nonetheless can play a decisive role in social interaction.'[9] Thus legal rights and formal structures of authority may be patriarchal, but the way a society actually functions at important levels may reflect the power of its women as much as the power of its men. It follows that, if, in observing such a society, one focuses on legal rights, formal positions in society and high-profile activities in the community, the society will appear more patriarchal than it really is.[10] The male perspective in such a society normally does focus on such aspects, and so it is only by adopting the women's perspective that one can see beyond the patriarchal structures to the more gender-balanced social reality.

Making Women Visible

The implication of Meyers' approach is that the predominantly androcentric texts of the Hebrew Bible, which foreground precisely the public life in which male authority is displayed, make Israelite society appear more patriarchal than in social reality it was. It renders invisible the real independence, initiative and power which women exercised within the household and the aspects of relationship in which women and men interacted in more egalitarian than hierarchical terms. The value of Ruth as women's literature is precisely that it renders visible what is usually invisible. Naomi and Ruth, as women of independence and initiative, respected as such by their men, are not exceptions to the Israelite rule. They are examples of the rule which the women's perspective unusually afforded us by this book allows us to recognize.

So, returning once again to the story, we can see how it is the structures of patriarchal authority which operate in the scene at the city gate which gives us the male perspective on events (4.1-12). Here, where legal rights and procedures

---

8   Meyers, *Discovering Eve*, p 43.
9   Ibid p 41, following M Z Rosaldo.
10 Ibid pp 42-45.

are at issue, the men manage everything, and the structures operate to secure male interests in patrilineal inheritance and descent. In this scene there is no hint at all that Boaz's marriage to Ruth in fact results from the initiatives taken by Naomi and by Ruth in the preceding chapter. It would be quite out of place in this scene where the women are mentioned only to have their affairs transacted by the men. Nor is there any indication of the significance which the women of Bethlehem subsequently see in the fruit of Boaz's union with Ruth (4.13-17). Naomi's economic security is not an explicit concern of the legal transaction at the gate, where the redemption of her land is designed to keep it within the kinship group by securing it for Elimelech's male heirs. Naomi's economic security is an effect of the transaction but not one to which the patriarchal form of the legal process explicitly attends. Thus the scene at the city gate shows us how male-dominated and neglectful of women's interests the story would seem if we saw it only from this male perspective. The surrounding narrative reveals what this male perspective leaves out: the initiative of the women, without which these events would not be taking place, and the way that the events serve the real interests of the women as well as the men.

4
The Genealogical Conclusion

Before we draw any firm conclusions about the importance of the women's perspective of the book of Ruth within the Bible as a whole, it is important to consider the way the book concludes. The story itself ends in the middle of verse 17 of chapter 4, when the women of Bethlehem, having declared the child of Ruth and Boaz to be Naomi's son, name him Obed. Here the story itself ends, but a comment is added (the conclusion of verse 17) which connects the narrative with the biblical history familiar to its readers by informing us that Obed was the grandfather of king David. Read in the light of the preceding narrative, of course, this comment traces David's ancestry back through Ruth to Naomi, since the levirate marriage of Ruth to Boaz made her son legally heir to her first husband Mahlon, the son of Naomi and Elimelech. So the women's perspective is continued even in this genealogical conclusion to verse 17.

However, verse 17 is not the end of the book. In verses 18-22 the book concludes with a formally constructed genealogy tracing David's descent from Perez the son of the patriarch Judah. It has often been thought that this is a later addition to the book, but there is really no way of knowing this. Whether or not it was added to the narrative by the book's original author or by a later editor is in fact of little importance, since it unquestionably forms part of the final form of the book of Ruth which is the book as we have it in Scripture. Its role in relation to the narrative is the important question. Modern western readers of Scripture rarely pay much attention to genealogies, but for ancient readers genealogies were interesting and important. If we dismiss this genealogy as an uninteresting appendix to Ruth we shall miss something important about the way the book presents a women's perspective on ancient Israelite society.

Three general points about biblical genealogies will help us to understand the significance of this one. First, genealogies always trace the male line of descent from father to son. This corresponds to the patrilineal principle of inheritance in ancient Israel. Women appear in genealogies occasionally as mothers (especially if a man had two wives and his sons by each wife are distinguished) or as sisters of the men listed, but the line of descent is never traced through a woman. Therefore a genealogy which traces a single line of descent, without collateral branches, as this one does, consists only of male names. This genealogy traces David's descent in the male line from Perez. It corresponds to 1 Chronicles 2.5-15, but excludes the non-essential information found there. As a typical Israelite patrilineal genealogy it makes no mention of Ruth, let alone Naomi.

Secondly, since ancient Israelites thought of historical time as the succession of generations, rather than, as we do, in chronological periods such as centuries, a genealogy can serve as a summary of a period of history. Israelite readers would recognize this genealogy as one which spans a long period of Israelite history: from the entry into Egypt to the beginning of the monarchy.

Thirdly, the numerical features of genealogies are often important. In this case, there are ten generations (as in, for example, the line from Shem to Abraham in Gen 11.10-26), making David, in the tenth generation, a climax. But the most significant place in the genealogy is the seventh (cf Enoch 'the seventh from Adam:' Jude 14; Gen 5.1-18), which is occupied by Boaz. This is why the genealogy begins with Perez, rather than, as one might have expected, his much more important father Judah, who would have indicated the tribal affiliation of the whole line of descent. By starting with Perez, the genealogy is able to place Boaz in the all-important seventh position. To this extent the genealogy has been framed so as to connect with the story of the book of Ruth. It highlights that male figure in the genealogy of David's ancestry who features in the story.

Connexions with the Story of Ruth

However, it is striking that this highlighting of Boaz, by virtue of his position in seventh place, is the only way in which the genealogy is connected with the story of the book. David's ancestry is not traced through Mahlon and Elimelech, as Ruth's levirate marriage, making her son by Boaz legally Mahlon's heir, might seem to require, but through Boaz. The way the story has told us that Boaz came to father Obed is left entirely out of account in the genealogy. The reason for this lack of connection with the story is no doubt that the genealogy is no more than an extract from a traditional genealogy of David, such as also appears in 1 Chronicles 2. The extract was made—by starting with Perez—in such as way as to place Boaz seventh, but it has not otherwise been adapted to the story of Ruth.

As an extract from a traditional Israelite genealogy, summarizing history by means of a purely male line of descent, this genealogical conclusion to Ruth departs from the women's perspective which the book's narrative has adopted and with which it very emphatically ended in 4.17. Instead it adopts the thoroughly male perspective of a patrilineal genealogy. The effect is to contrast the story, told from a women's perspective, with the male perspective of the genealogy which is representative of most Old Testament historiography. The genealogy says in effect: 'This is how the usual men's perspective views the history of this period of David's ancestors. This is the way you readers are accustomed to thinking of this period. Everything the narrative you have just read has taught you to see as important is here left out.' Readers who have truly appreciated the women's perspective afforded them by the story of Ruth are bound to find the genealogical conclusion pitifully inadequate in its androcentric selectivity. The narrative and the genealogy purport to recount the same history, but the women's world of the narrative is left wholly invisible by the male line of succession which the genealogy records. Thus the book of Ruth, its conclusion tells us, is the kind of story which official, masculine history leaves out.

Ruth's Canonical Role

The genealogy could be regarded as representing all the androcentric narratives of the Hebrew Bible. Readers of Ruth who know such texts will already, before reaching the genealogy, have been constantly aware of the contrast between its female perspective and the male perspective of these other scriptural narratives. The book's effect on them will have been to expose by contrast the androcentricity of these other texts. Seeing the women's perspective on Israelite society in this case brings home how far it is absent in other cases. But then the effect of the genealogical conclusion to Ruth is to bring this contrast between the gynocentricity of Ruth and the androcentricity of other Old Testament narratives within the structure of the book itself. In this way the book itself gives itself the role of supplying the women's perspective which most Israelite narrative, represented by the genealogy, leaves out and of exposing the inadequacy of the purely androcentric perspective of such texts as the genealogy represents.

In effect this gives Ruth an important canonical function, that is, a function in relation to the rest of the contents of the canon of Scripture, or, in this case, in relation to the other narratives in Scripture. By revealing the Israelite women's world which is elsewhere invisible in biblical narrative it makes readers aware of the lack of this women's perspective elsewhere and it also authorizes them to supply just such a women's perspective elsewhere, expanding the hints and filling in the gaps which they can now see to be left by the narratives written purely or largely from a male perspective.

5

Women's Perspectives Elsewhere in Biblical Narrative

The Book of Ruth is a sustained presentation of a women's perspective, offering a clear contrast between this perspective and a male perspective, and written with a literary artistry which draws readers into the world as seen through Naomi's and Ruth's eyes. For these reasons it can play a special role, within the canon of Scripture, in awakening readers to the issue of gender perspective in biblical narrative. It can make us more conscious of the androcentrism of other narratives. But it can also draw our attention to other instances where this androcentrism is interrupted by a women's perspective.

We might look again, for example, at the stories of the patriarchs and the matriarchs in Genesis. The fact that we habitually think of these as the stories of the patriarchs reflects the male bias of traditional interpretation. But it is not entirely untrue to the stories themselves, in which Abraham, Isaac, Jacob and his sons are more prominent than Sarah, Rebekah, Leah, Rachel and Dinah. But there are passages where the narrative adopts the perspective of the female characters (eg 16; 21.6-21; 29.31-30.24). Sensitive reading of these passages can open up the women's perspective, not only within the passages themselves, but in such a way as to throw light on their androcentric contexts. With some imagination we can begin to read the whole narrative from the women's perspective, as well as from the perspective of the men which the narrative itself adopts for much of the time.

The Gospel Birth Narratives

A striking New Testament example of a gynocentric narrative is the first two chapters of Luke's Gospel. Although the perspectives of male characters—Zechariah, the shepherds, Simeon—are included, the dominant perspectives are those of Elizabeth and Mary. We are taken into the private thoughts of these two women (1.25; 2.19, 51). A key scene in the narrative is one in which the two women are alone together (1.39-56). (Scenes in which women characters act and converse without any men present are integral to the book of Ruth's depiction of a women's perspective, but they are rare elsewhere in the biblical narratives. In a scene where women are with men, a narrator may portray the women from a male perspective. But a scene in which only women are present is more likely to be a narrator's attempt to enter the women's world on its own terms.) The female perspective of Luke's birth narratives is in striking contrast to Matthew's birth and infancy narrative (1.18-2.23), which adopts wholly the perspective of the male characters: Joseph, Herod and the wise men. In Matthew's narrative

Mary never speaks and is never addressed by another character.

The reason for this contrast is important. Matthew's narrative is concerned with the political sphere, in which Jesus is heir to the throne of David (necessarily inherited through the male line of his adoptive father Joseph), is acknowledged as such by the wise men, and is the victim of Herod's suspicious fear for his own political survival. The family's travels as political refugees are the kind of affairs of which, in this society, men take charge. Matthew's narrative moves in the public, political world where male authority rules, just as Luke's does for those few verses (2.1-5) in which political authority, taxation and lineage take a necessary part in the plot. But Luke's dominantly female perspective corresponds to the domestic setting of the household in which much of his narrative is set.

Luke's Domestic Setting

In Matthew's narrative Mary of course plays the all-important role of giving birth to Jesus. But the significance of the birth is played out in the activities of the male characters in the public, political sphere. In Luke, by contrast, the significance of the birth of Jesus is seen predominantly from the perspective of the two women, especially Mary. Moreover, the women appear as agents, initiating and acting in the working out of their own destiny and that of others. Mary in particular is the key human agent in the story as Luke tells it. Here we see, as in Ruth, the contrast between the official sphere of male authority, in which women appear only so that the men can manage their affairs, and the informal sphere of female power, the household, where the women have significant independence and effects. Only a gynocentric narrative like Luke's reveals the latter, while androcentric narratives like Matthew's leave it invisible. By entering the domestic setting, in which Mary's acceptance of her God-given role as mother of the Lord can be portrayed at length (1.26-56), Luke's narrative presents Mary as an agent of God's deliverance of his people, comparable with such Old Testament figures as Moses, Joshua and Deborah. While these figures acted for God in the public, political sphere (Deborah is an unusual biblical instance of a woman doing so in the same way as a man), Mary's role, as mother, takes place within the household, the sphere in which traditionally women could influence events as decisively as men did. The authentically female perspective appears especially in the fact that Mary's role can certainly not be seen as *confined to* the household. It is through her agency that God deposes the powerful from their thrones and exalts the lowly, fills the hungry and deprives the rich, delivers his people and fulfils the promises to Abraham (1.52-55). Mary's response to God within the women's world of the household is of decisive effect on human history and all of human life. Mary's role in God's purpose breaks through the distinction between the domestic sphere where women have influence and the public sphere where they largely do not. As mother of the Lord, she proves to be a new and greater Deborah, in a public and political sense 'a mother in Israel' (Judg 5.7).

IS THE BIBLE MALE?

Jesus' Ministry and Passion

For a final example of the way women's perspectives may be found in bibli-cal narratives we turn to the major parts of the Gospels, which recount Jesus' ministry and passion. A literary characteristic of the stories about Jesus in the Gospels which is often neglected is that, for the most part, these stories do not invite their readers to adopt Jesus' perspective on the events. Much more often they invite their readers to adopt successively the many different perspectives of the people who hear, observe, encounter and follow Jesus. The perspective may be the collective perspective of crowds or disciples, but frequently it is the perspective of one of the many individuals who interact with Jesus in narratives of healing or discipleship or other forms of encounter. Many of these individu-als, of course, are women: women who follow Jesus as disciples along with the male disciples; women who welcome Jesus into their homes; women who come to him for healing for themselves or others. In many of these stories the wom-en's perspective is not developed at length by the narrative, because the Gospel stories are characteristically spare narratives, which outline and suggest rather than exhaustively portraying. They invite readers to enter imaginatively into them and, in these cases, to use their own imagination in adopting the women's perspective on Jesus and the events.

In these stories Jesus interacts with women most often within the household or in synagogues, less often in the public places where many of his encounters with men occur (but cf Mark 5.24-34; Luke 11.28; John 4.7-30). These were a predominantly, though certainly not exclusively, male world, but Jesus does not move only in this world of male dominance. He is often to be seen in the spheres in which women were active and influential. The scenes which portray his friend-ship with the sisters Martha and Mary are particularly notable (Luke 10.38-42; John 11.1-44; 12.1-8). Some interpretation of the women in the Gospels has tended to exaggerate the restrictions placed on women by Jewish society of the time, in order to play up, by contrast, the independent and prominent roles which women played in the ministry of Jesus and the early church. It is probably more appro-priate to notice that the Jewish literature on which this view is based is androcentric literature, portraying women in the strictly subordinate role they have from the point of view of the patriarchal structures of male authority. The book of Ruth has already taught us to discount the onesidedness of this androcentric perspective. It makes Jewish society look more patriarchal than it really was, because it views women from the perspective of those aspects of society where men dominated. Some of the Gospel stories, on the other hand, show us Jewish women from their own point of view, exercising the initiative and independence which the real dynamics of such a society did allow them. For the most part the women in the Gospels do not step outside the traditional social roles of women in their society, but they sometimes show us the extent to which women were active subjects of their own lives and influential on others' within their traditional sphere of the household.

The Church in the Household

This is not to say that the women in the Gospels never behave in socially unusual ways. Mary, sitting at Jesus' feet like the disciple of a rabbi, learning her master's teaching in order to become a teacher herself (Luke 10.38-42), is perhaps the most striking example. Although there were women disciples who accompanied Jesus in his itinerant ministry (Luke 8.2-3), it is worth noticing that this example of Mary behaving in a way indistinguishable from male disciples of Jewish teachers takes place in a domestic setting. It foreshadows the way that in the earliest Christian churches women played roles of leadership and teaching which were relatively non-traditional roles for women. This prominence of women should be associated with the fact that the household was in many respects the setting of the early Christian movement. Within their traditional sphere of activity and influence, early Christian women could more easily adopt relatively non-traditional roles. The early Christian movement was inevitably constrained to some degree by the patriarchal structure of the societies in which it moved, but it exploited to the full the space that structure left for women to play prominent roles. By making their sphere, the household, into, as it were, the Christian public space, it could give women roles which were not allowed them in the non-Christian public world of the market place, the city gate, and the temple. So, in those Gospel stories which adopt the women's perspective in a domestic setting, we can trace a line of continuity from Naomi and Ruth, through Elizabeth and Mary the mother of Jesus, through the women who entertained Jesus in their homes and became his disciples, and on to the prominent women of the early church, such as Priscilla and Junia. Tracing this female trajectory depends upon entering fully into the women's perspective of those gynocentric parts of the biblical narratives which so powerfully interrupt the more dominant androcentricity.

6
Conclusion

In conclusion, an important point may need to be made, in order to counter a possible misunderstanding. The biblical narratives depict a patriarchal society (or a series of patriarchal societies) with accepted gender roles (even if these were not as inflexible and watertight as is sometimes imagined). Men have official authority in the public sphere; women have real power and influence, alongside men, in the domestic sphere. We have seen that, if one enters into the women's perspective on this society which the biblical narratives sometimes afford us, it looks less patriarchal than the androcentric narratives which portray it from the male perspective might suggest. But there is no doubt that it is patriarchal, assigns gender roles, and gives men rights and privileges women do not have. It has been no part of the purpose of this discussion to vindicate the patriarchal structures and gender roles of biblical societies as normative for today. Patriarchalism as such has not been the issue we have addressed. A quite different hermeneutical approach would be needed to do so.

What we have done is to illustrate the way biblical narratives do afford us the perspective of women within the biblical societies, as well as that of men. That there are clear differences of perspective results, of course, largely from the fact that these societies were patriarchal societies in which men and women played different roles and therefore viewed the world from differing (though naturally also overlapping) perspectives. For us to adopt either the male or the female perspective is an exercise in entering imaginatively into the world which the biblical texts portray for us. As readers of Scripture it is essential to do this. The texts invite us to do so. It is how narratives engage and affect their readers.

Perspective and Role Models

However, this does not mean that, as modern readers of Scripture, men should identify with the male characters and their androcentric perspective, while women should identify with the female characters and their gynocentric perspective. Androcentric and gynocentric perspectives are culturally relative. The structures of biblical societies, including the gender roles, are not those of today. The distinction between the domestic and the public spheres, for example, is quite different in modern western societies from what it was in ancient Israel. We could not reproduce the gender roles of ancient Israel in modern society, even if we wished to. Therefore contemporary Christian women will not necessarily find in the social situations and attitudes of biblical women more correspondence to their own situation than they find in the case of biblical men. There is no good reason why, for example, the women disciples of Jesus should be role models only for Christian women today and the male disciples of Jesus role models only for Christian men. Disciples of both sexes can be role models (and warning examples!) for Christians of both sexes today.

With this essential qualification, it is nevertheless important for women readers of Scripture today to appreciate the extent to which the perspective of the women members of the people of God in biblical times is available to us within the biblical narratives. It is important also for men as readers of Scripture to be freed from the androcentric prejudices which professional male interpretation of Scripture has tended to promote. The Bible is the Word of God in the words of men and women. In its narratives it conveys God's message by drawing us into the perspectives of its characters. That of the male characters alone is one-sided, distorted by the patriarchal structures of their society. As one human perspective it can convey God's message adequately only if we supplement and correct it from the alternative perspective of the biblical women. Even though the majority of biblical narratives are androcentric, there are enough authentically gynocentric narratives to counteract this dominant androcentricity, provided we allow them to do so.

I have concentrated on explaining in detail the way the book of Ruth offers a deliberate gynocentric alternative and correction to the androcentricity characteristic of Old Testament narrative. I have gone on to suggest the way in which a hermeneutical approach learned from Ruth can be carried through in relation to other biblical narratives. I have left much for readers to do for themselves. Once awakened to the difference between men's and women's perspectives in biblical narratives, sensitive and imaginative readers will find themselves reading many texts with new eyes—those of the biblical women.

Appendix
A Note on Literature

My approach to reading Ruth is presented in a somewhat different way in my article: 'The Book of Ruth and the Possibility of a Feminist Canonical Hermeneutic' (forthcoming in the journal *Biblical Interpretation*).

For recovering the women's perspectives in Old Testament narratives, there is valuable material in many of the essays collected in the ten volumes of Athalya Brenner (ed), *A Feminist Companion to the Bible* (Sheffield: Sheffield Academic Press, 1993-1996). My argument is indebted to some of the essays in the volume on Ruth (vol 3). On Esther and Ruth, see also André LaCocque, *The Feminine Unconventional* (Minneapolis: Fortress, 1990). On Genesis, see also Sharon Pace Jeansonne, *The Women of Genesis* (Minneapolis: Fortress, 1990).

Though the approach I have advocated is not exactly to be found in any of the recent literature about women in the Gospels, the following books, among others, may help in the task of entering the women's perspective in Gospel narratives: Carla Ricci, *Mary Magdalene and Many Others*, tr P Burns (Minneapolis: Fortress, 1994); Elizabeth Moltmann-Wendel, *The Women around Jesus*, tr J Bowden (London: SCM Press, 1982); Turid Karlsen Seim, *The Double Message: Patterns of Gender in Luke-Acts* (Edinburgh: T & T Clark, 1994); Hisako Kinukawa, *Women and Jesus in Mark: A Japanese Feminist Perspective* (New York: Orbis, 1994); Luise Schottroff, *Lydia's Impatient Sisters: A Feminist Social History of Early Christianity* (London: SCM Press, 1995).